Prophets of *Zoom*

This book is dedicated to the memory
of John Gorham and Alan Fletcher,
who helped in its early development
but sadly did not see it published.

# Prophets of *Zoom*

Alfredo Marcantonio

MERRELL
LONDON · NEW YORK

The World of Tomorrow

Throughout the first half of the twentieth century Britain was awash with collectors' cards. The manufacturers of everything from tea to tobacco produced sets of cards featuring flora, fauna, footballers and film stars, with the objective of encouraging people to repurchase their products and of building what today's marketing folk call 'brand loyalty'.

In the mid-1930s, with the card craze reaching its peak, the directors of Stephen Mitchell & Son, a small Scottish cigarette maker, joined the fray. They commissioned what is surely one of the most imaginative sets of all: *The World of Tomorrow*, a series of fifty cards that set out to forecast the future. The series was the result of a collaboration with Idrisyn Oliver Evans, a collectors' card enthusiast who had recently compiled a book of the same title.

A glance at the cards quickly reveals that these 'Prophets of Zoom' were inspired not simply by science fiction, but also by cinema. Contemporary films, including Alexander Korda's *Things to Come* (1936), as well as *High Treason* (1928), *Just Imagine* (1930) and *The Tunnel* (1935), provided several of the images for Evans's visions.

A number of cards were inspired by the inventions of the electrical engineer and physicist Nikola Tesla, while others feature photographs of what was clearly cutting-edge technology at the time. This latter group includes the Grundtvig Church in Copenhagen, Erich Mendelsohn's Einstein Tower in Potsdam, the John Fowler 'Gyrotiller' and the urban architecture of Le Corbusier.

The individual predictions range from the amusing to the amazing. Together they paint a unique picture of the world we live in now, as pre-war Britain imagined it would look.

In addition to showcasing the cards, this book sets out to demonstrate just how accurate, or inaccurate, the various forecasts have proved to be. Opposite each of the cards we have reproduced a contemporary image of our own choosing.

In some instances – such as card 5, the 'Wind Turbine Station' – we have attempted to track down a modern-day, state-of-the-art equivalent. Where this has proved to be impossible, we have chosen to use artistic and, on occasion, comedic licence. There is irony aplenty to be enjoyed over the pages that follow.

Mr Evans and co. clearly anticipated remarkable advances in civil engineering: card 32 sees Britain joined to mainland Europe, thanks to a bit of nifty 'North Sea Reclamation'. Similarly, card 34 sees Spain joined to Africa, with the Mediterranean neatly separated from the mighty Atlantic courtesy of the 'Gibraltar Dam'.

This confidence in our ability to conquer the sea wasn't matched in the sky. These 'Prophets of Zoom' could not imagine that advances in aeronautical engineering might one day enable an aircraft to cross that very ocean without having to touch down for fuel. As a result, card 19 sees us creating the 'Mid-Ocean Airport', a form of structure that did eventually grace the seas, not to dispense fuel but to harvest it from the seabed.

With the First World War a recent memory, a number of the cards raise the threat of gas and chemicals being used as weapons. It was a spectre that was to haunt the Allies throughout the Second World War, and it is a horror that remains a real threat to this day.

In stark contrast, card 6 sees the authors in optimistic mood. It illustrates an 'Atomic Disintegrator', heralding the splitting of the atom, but happily foreseeing only positive uses for 'the vast stores of energy' that might be unleashed.

Even more charmingly, card 42 acknowledges the need for ever-swifter communications, and envisages not the telex, not the fax, but 'Rocket Post'; thanks to email, the need for speed has been satisfied not by touchpaper but by touch-typing.

As one leafs through this book, seventy years after these cards were created, such subjects as 'Rocket Post' appear laughable. Yet one need look no further than the opening sentence on the back of the very first card, 'Solar Motor', to see that some of the cards' prophecies were chillingly accurate: 'Coal-mines and oil-wells will not last for ever. We shall have to gain the energy we need, not from fuel, but from the inexhaustible forces of nature.' Would that the world had taken note.

Alfredo Marcantonio

Prophets of *Zoom*

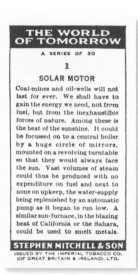

1
SOLAR MOTOR

The very first sentence on this very first card represents the most telling forecast of all. The text that follows proved to be equally prophetic: there is a solar furnace at Odeillo Font-Romeu in the French Pyrenees, and this impressive 650,000-panel installation is sited, just as the writer imagined, in California, at Kramer Junction.

A SERIES OF 50

2

## TIDAL POWER GENERATOR

In the tides of the sea we have a possible source of energy which now goes almost completely unused. There are several methods by which it could be tapped. Huge floats could be made, connected by levers to a train of gear-wheels by which they could be made to drive dynamos. Small though their rise and fall would be between high and low tide, the power that heavy floats would exert would be great indeed. Elsewhere the tides might ebb and flow through channels into inland basins, driving water-turbines like those used to-day to harness the mountain torrents. River-mouths and bays might similarly be shut in by huge barricades to trap the tidal waters.

STEPHEN MITCHELL & SON

ISSUED BY THE IMPERIAL TOBACCO CO.
(OF GREAT BRITAIN & IRELAND), LTD.

MITCHELL'S CIGARETTES

TIDAL POWER GENERATOR

2
## TIDAL POWER GENERATOR

It would be thirty years before the tide was harnessed by this barrier in the Rance Estuary, near Saint-Malo in northern France. Until recently it was one of only a few such schemes. Today more than twenty are under consideration: some are estuary-based; others employ submerged turbines that sit offshore.

SEA POWER GENERATOR

3
SEA POWER GENERATOR

This card depicts Ocean Thermal Energy Conversion (OTEC), which was pioneered by a number of physicists as long ago as the 1880s. A floating OTEC facility is currently being trialled off the coast of India. Pictured opposite is a major OTEC installation on the Kona Coast of Hawaii.

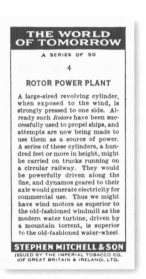

A SERIES OF 50

4

ROTOR POWER PLANT

A large-sized revolving cylinder, when exposed to the wind, is strongly pressed to one side. Already such *Rotors* have been successfully used to propel ships, and attempts are now being made to use them as a source of power. A series of these cylinders, a hundred feet or more in height, might be carried on trucks running on a circular railway. They would be powerfully driven along the line, and dynamos geared to their axle would generate electricity for commercial use. Thus we might have wind motors as superior to the old-fashioned windmill as the modern water turbine, driven by a mountain torrent, is superior to the old-fashioned water-wheel.

STEPHEN MITCHELL & SON

ISSUED BY THE IMPERIAL TOBACCO CO.
(OF GREAT BRITAIN & IRELAND), LTD.

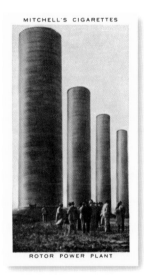

MITCHELL'S CIGARETTES

ROTOR POWER PLANT

4
ROTOR POWER PLANT

Today the wind creates electricity via a spinning blade rather than a revolving cylinder. A similar structure did, however, harness an air current of its own making: heated by solar panels, the rising warm air inside the short-lived 200-metre (656-foot) Manzares solar tower in Spain drove a series of turbines.

5

WIND TURBINE STATION

Winds high above the earth are both stronger and more constant than those nearer the ground, and in them we have a possible source of energy as yet completely untapped. The German engineer Hermann Honnef suggests the erection of a wind power station 1,500 feet high, built of a steel framework and carrying a number of gigantic wind vanes. These would be connected direct to dynamos, carrying current to the transformer stations at the foot of the tower, from which it would be transmitted over the land.

STEPHEN MITCHELL & SON

ISSUED BY THE IMPERIAL TOBACCO CO. (OF GREAT BRITAIN & IRELAND), LTD.

MITCHELL'S CIGARETTES

WIND TURBINE STATION

5
WIND TURBINE STATION
This prediction has proved to be accurate in terms of function rather than form. The complicated steel pylon is now a sleek pillar; in place of several vanes there are just a few slender blades; and at a height of some 118 metres (390 feet), the modern turbine falls a long way short of the 457 metres (1500 feet) envisaged.

A SERIES OF 50

6

## ATOMIC DISINTEGRATOR

Attempts have recently been made to "split the atom." Though these have not so far been very spectacular, nor have had any practical application, their theoretical results have been important. Developments of similar methods might enable us to release the vast stores of energy which are thought to hold the atom together, thus obtaining unlimited supplies of power for our use. Further advances in this work might also enable us to break down the more complicated atoms into the more simple, so converting common elements into those of which we are in need, and overcoming any possible shortage of food supplies, or raw materials for our industries.

**STEPHEN MITCHELL & SON**

ISSUED BY THE IMPERIAL TOBACCO CO. (OF GREAT BRITAIN & IRELAND) LTD.

MITCHELL'S CIGARETTES

ATOMIC DISINTEGRATOR

6
## ATOMIC DISINTEGRATOR

By the time this card was printed, successful attempts had indeed been made to split the atom. A decade later 'vast stores of energy' were being harnessed by Enrico Fermi's prototype power station in Chicago. Less than twenty years after that, work had begun on this futuristic French reactor at Avoine-Chinon on the Loire.

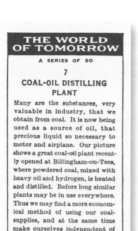

MITCHELL'S CIGARETTES

COAL-OIL DISTILLING PLANT

7
COAL-OIL DISTILLING PLANT

The card's 'coal-oil plant' at Billingham in the north-east of England was closed in 1994, but the Fischer–Tropsch
process that it exploited so successfully lives on. Shell uses similar technology to create fuel from natural
gas here at Bintulu in Malaysia. Elsewhere it is used to transform natural gas into Shell's GTL (gas-to-liquid) fuel.

## MECHANICAL EXCAVATOR

In place of hand labour with pick and shovel, the mining of the future might make use of immense mechanical excavators, ripping away vast masses of rock. They would squirt chemicals into the rocks to dissolve part of their minerals into inflammable gas. Then an electric flash could be applied by means of great rods of carbon, and the rocks would blow themselves to pieces. Cabins of steel and toughened glass would protect the "crews" of the excavators from the force of the explosion and from falling pieces of rock. (*Photograph by courtesy of London Film Productions, Ltd., from the film "Things to Come"*).

**STEPHEN MITCHELL & SON**

ISSUED BY THE IMPERIAL TOBACCO CO.
(OF GREAT BRITAIN & IRELAND), LTD.

MITCHELL'S CIGARETTES

MECHANICAL EXCAVATOR

8
MECHANICAL EXCAVATOR

It was the boring of the Channel Tunnel, not the mining of inaccessible minerals, that spawned the creation of the mechanical excavator par excellence. Some 200 metres (656 feet) long and weighing 580 tonnes, it succeeded without 'chemicals' or 'explosions' by employing technology that was truly cutting-edge.

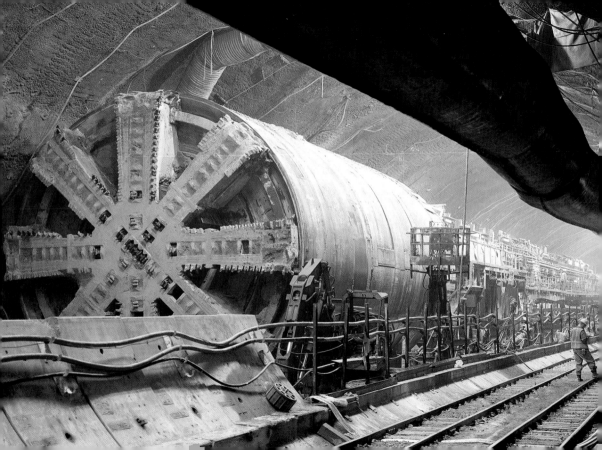

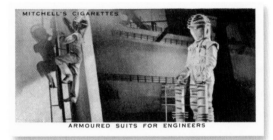

MITCHELL'S CIGARETTES

ARMOURED SUITS FOR ENGINEERS

9
ARMOURED SUITS FOR ENGINEERS

Sadly it is the peacekeeper, not the engineer, who needs such highly protective clothing.
Violent crime has made body armour a standard item of police uniform. In addition, terrorism has
led not only to the 'armoured suit' becoming a reality but also to the bomb-disposal robot.

OFFICE OF THE FUTURE

## 10
### OFFICE OF THE FUTURE

The ecclesiastical architecture is a bit wide of the mark, and so are the uniforms. But the notion of massed ranks of workers has proved to be remarkably accurate, as has the talk of 'intricate machines', 'television screens' and 'conditioned and warmed' air.

11

## STREAM-LINED TRAIN

Experiments made with stream-lined railway engines and trains show a marked increase in efficiency and a reduction in running-cost. The trains of the future, engine and carriages alike, might be surrounded by a stream-lined covering, free from any projections or other irregularities that would offer needless resistance to the air, but flexible for rounding curves. Windows and ventilators would thus need to be built flush with the carriage walls. In place of wheels the train might run on giant ball-bearings, so as to reduce friction still further or, instead of travelling on rails just above the surface of the ground, it might move along a smooth trough excavated below ground-level.

STEPHEN MITCHELL & SON

ISSUED BY THE IMPERIAL TOBACCO CO.
(OF GREAT BRITAIN & IRELAND), LTD.

MITCHELL'S CIGARETTES

STREAM-LINED TRAIN

11
STREAM-LINED TRAIN

The 1964 launch of the 200-km/h (125-mph) Tokyo–Osaka bullet train transformed this fantasy into fact. Ever-faster versions have followed. The foreseen 'flush' windows have appeared and, as predicted, the wheels have disappeared; in 2005 a 'hovering' magnetic prototype clocked over 580 km/h (360 mph).

# THE WORLD OF TOMORROW

A SERIES OF 50

12

RAILPLANE

Our present passenger trains may well be superseded by *Railplanes*, suspended from rails carried on lattice-girders well above the surface of the ground. Stream-lined, and propelled by motor-driven screws, they could reach speeds of over a hundred miles an hour and yet be safe and quite free from vibration or noise. The present-day ground lines could then be given over to goods traffic. Alternatively, the goods trains could be run underground in tubes, and the existing railroads could be re-surfaced for high-speed long-distance motor traffic.

**STEPHEN MITCHELL & SON**

ISSUED BY THE IMPERIAL TOBACCO CO. (OF GREAT BRITAIN & IRELAND) LTD.

MITCHELL'S CIGARETTES

RAILPLANE

## 12
### RAILPLANE

George Bennie's Railplane, conceived in the 1920s, never 'took off' in any sense of the term.
Monorails had wheezed overhead since the early 1900s; it was Disneyland that gave them a smooth, space-age image, an aesthetic now maintained by Shanghai's maglev monorail, the fastest train service in the world.

TUNNEL TRAVEL

13
TUNNEL TRAVEL

It would be sixty years before the tunnel was built below 'the Straits of Dover', complete with 'stream-lined electric trains' travelling 'at high speed'. Regrettably, the more fanciful vision of a 'transatlantic tunnel', linking Britain to America, remains no more than a pipe dream.

MITCHELL'S CIGARETTES

ROAD LINER

14
ROAD LINER

Dismissed as wasteful of space, streamlining as flamboyant as this never caught on. Inside, however,
the 'kitchens' have to some extent materialized, as have the 'cinema' and 'wireless'. There are
toilets, too, but with motorway speeds of 113 km/h (70 mph), the 'sun-deck' has proved to be over the top.

To-day stream-lined motors and trains are beginning to be built, with the result that their speed and ease of running are increased and their friction and fuel-consumption lessened. Equally good results may be gained when ships (even the great transatlantic liners) are stream-lined. Deck, bridge and upper works would be curved to reduce the resistance of the air, while the hull would form a hydroplane, so that the ship would rise in the waves and decrease the water resistance. The ship's officers would keep their look-out, and the passengers would gaze, through windows of tough glass flush with the hull.

**STEPHEN MITCHELL & SON**

ISSUED BY THE IMPERIAL TOBACCO CO.
(OF GREAT BRITAIN & IRELAND), LTD.

MITCHELL'S CIGARETTES

STREAM-LINED SPEED-SHIP

## 15
### STREAM-LINED SPEED-SHIP

As well as providing another eulogy on streamlining, this shipping forecast includes the 'hydroplane', technology now used by smaller ferries the world over. And while larger craft do indeed 'rise in the waves and decrease the water resistance', it is the catamaran hull rather than the hydrofoil that is usually responsible.

MITCHELL'S CIGARETTES

FOG ELIMINATOR

16
FOG ELIMINATOR

Infrared and heat detection are with us, but 'a beam of clearness through the swirling mists' remains elusive. 'Radio Detection And Ranging', Radar, appeared soon after this card was issued and became a vital weapon, not just against fog but also against all manner of other malevolent forces.

ONE-MAN SUBMARINE

Already the Japanese are said to have experimented with "human torpedoes" in which a sailor travels to steer a cargo of high explosive against its target. These would be useful enough in war, and such one-man submarines may equally have a more peaceful use in reaching depths too great for an ordinary diver. These craft might do good work in mapping out the sea-floor, searching for submarine mineral beds, exploring wrecks and, possibly, in fishing for the strange creatures which live far below the waves. Equipped with powerful motors and with stores of fuel, food, and compressed air, they would greatly aid scientific research and form a new sport.

STEPHEN MITCHELL & SON

ISSUED BY THE IMPERIAL TOBACCO CO.
(OF GREAT BRITAIN & IRELAND), LTD.

MITCHELL'S CIGARETTES

ONE-MAN SUBMARINE

17
ONE-MAN SUBMARINE

Built as weapons of war for more than 150 years, submarines had an illustrious history and would come into their own in the Second World War. Today's 'DeepWorker 2000' is a constructive rather than a destructive vehicle, designed to carry out rescues and repairs at up to 610 metres (2000 feet) below sea level.

MITCHELL'S CIGARETTES

SUPER-AIRPLANE

18
SUPER-AIRPLANE

The projected span of the wings is about right, but their predicted shape is wide of the mark. In place of eight prop engines there are four giant jets, and while the frame of this 850-seater is indeed 'built entirely of metal', it weighs just half the estimated 'thousand tons'.

MITCHELL'S CIGARETTES

MID-OCEAN AIRPORT

19
MID-OCEAN AIRPORT

Oddly, the writer foresees engineers who are capable of building an entire airport in the middle of the Atlantic Ocean, yet incapable of building a plane that could fly across it. A similar structure has, of course, graced the seas, not for the distribution of fuel but for its collection.

MITCHELL'S CIGARETTES

COMPOSITE AIRCRAFT

20
COMPOSITE AIRCRAFT

Fuel consumption was the motivator for this piece of blue-sky thinking. Unlikely as it seems,
this composite aircraft consisting of two flying boats was actually built, by Short Brothers, and history
repeated itself in the late 1970s, when NASA's first Space Shuttle underwent its flight trials.

21

## HIGH LEVEL AIRPORT

As airplane traffic increases, the great cities feel a growing need for central airports situated in their midst. This need could be met by the construction of a high-level airport, a concrete landing-field built two hundred feet above the docks or business houses. Shipping, railways and road traffic would pass beneath it, and its great supporting pillars could be honeycombed with offices and stores, and provided with lifts and escalators. This huge platform would not merely allow air traffic to alight and take off in a central position, but would also protect the vital centres of the city from air attack in wartime.

**STEPHEN MITCHELL & SON**

ISSUED BY THE IMPERIAL TOBACCO CO.
(OF GREAT BRITAIN & IRELAND), LTD.

MITCHELL'S CIGARETTES

HIGH LEVEL AIRPORT

21
HIGH LEVEL AIRPORT

In the 1960s and 1970s you could fly into the midst of Manhattan: a heliport on the
Pan Am Building ferried in passengers from nearby LaGuardia and JFK airports. Safety concerns following
an accident led to its closure in 1977; as we can see, they have no such worries in São Paulo, Brazil.

## 22
### TELEVISION

With early TV screens requiring the viewer to use magnifying lenses, 'pocket' television wasn't as radical
as it sounds. Colour was logical, too, but a large public screen, like this one in Tokyo's Shinjuku district, was a
truly inspired idea, with credit due to the screenwriter every bit as much as to the cardwriter.

MITCHELL'S CIGARETTES

NEW YORK OF THE FUTURE

23
NEW YORK OF THE FUTURE
New York's skyscrapers did not rise to the 'still greater heights' depicted.
In fact, the tragic destruction in 2001 of the World Trade Center re-established the 1930s Empire State Building as the city's tallest structure, although it appears dwarfed in the right-hand foreground of the card.

LONDON OF THE FUTURE

24
LONDON OF THE FUTURE

In truth, it was not because of its clay subsoil that London did not 'care for super-skyscrapers' but rather
because of its firemen's ladders: until the 1950s few buildings were allowed to exceed their 30-metre (100-foot) elevation.
Today, buildings are several times that height, but the church spires are still there. So is Big Ben.

CROSS-SHAPED SKYSCRAPERS

25
CROSS-SHAPED SKYSCRAPERS

Within a dozen years of the issue of this card, similar blocks to these, 'set out
at regular intervals', were up and renting in Stuyvesant Town, New York;
inspired by M. Le Corbusier no doubt, but designed by Irwin Clavan and Gilmore Clarke.

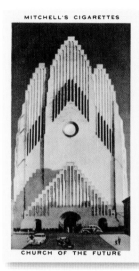

CHURCH OF THE FUTURE

26

CHURCH OF THE FUTURE

Architecture, like other forms of construction, is becoming "functional." It gains its beauty not from useless ornament added to suit the whim of the designer, but through its exact fitness for the purpose it has to fulfil. At the same time there is no reason why a building should not indicate by its outline the purpose for which it is intended. A novelty in church design is the edifice illustrated, which has recently been built in Copenhagen. Perhaps, instead of the tower or spire to which we are accustomed, this may become the habitual style by which we shall recognize our places of worship.

STEPHEN MITCHELL & SON

ISSUED BY THE IMPERIAL TOBACCO CO.
(OF GREAT BRITAIN & IRELAND), LTD.

26
CHURCH OF THE FUTURE

The writer of the card wonders if ecclesiastical architecture will see 'function' triumph over 'folly'.
The organ-like Grundtvig Church in Copenhagen clearly follows the latter route. Richard Meier's spare and graceful design for the Jubilee Church in Rome, however, pulls out all the stops in a very functional way.

**THE WORLD OF TOMORROW**

A SERIES OF 50

27

**REVOLVING HOUSE**

Every householder wants to get as much sunlight as possible for the living rooms of his dwelling. Here is an attempt to satisfy him— a house, pivoted to follow the sun in its daily journey across the sky. Driven by a small motor and running on tracks similar to railway lines, the house can be "set" to face any direction the occupant desires, or it can be geared, like the roof of an observatory, to compensate for the rotation of the earth. Experiments are being made with a house of this type in Italy, and such buildings may come to be regular features of all ambitious housing schemes.

**STEPHEN MITCHELL & SON**
ISSUED BY THE IMPERIAL TOBACCO CO.
(OF GREAT BRITAIN & IRELAND), LTD.

MITCHELL'S CIGARETTES

REVOLVING HOUSE

27
REVOLVING HOUSE

Angelo Invernizzi's Villa Girasole, near Verona, Italy, was circulating a year or so before these cards, but such houses remain a novelty. One recent example is Al and Janet Johnstone's rotating home in San Diego, California (2003); a multi-speed structure, it rotates on ball bearings, one of which is a full 2 metres (6½ feet) in diameter.

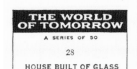

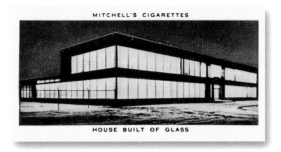

MITCHELL'S CIGARETTES

HOUSE BUILT OF GLASS

28
HOUSE BUILT OF GLASS

Ludwig Mies van der Rohe exhibited his glazed Barcelona Pavilion in 1929, years before this card's issue. In this house by Richard Rogers in London the pavilion's Bauhaus design has barely been improved upon, but its extensive glazing certainly has. Modern glass provides security, solar protection and insulation, all without becoming brick-thick, as described here.

HOUSE BUILDER

29
HOUSE BUILDER

The suggested steel framework and mechanical cranes do indeed dominate the construction of flats and offices, but house-building holds out. 'Paper' and 'plaster' remain popular; the precast panel has not dislodged the brick wall; and 'graceful curves' have failed to kill off 'dust-collecting corners'.

MITCHELL'S CIGARETTES

GYROTILLER

30
GYROTILLER

Modern monster tractors do have 'diesel motors' and can be equipped with 'tank-like' tracks, but all without resorting to gyroscopes for stability. The anticipated 'great blades' are added on rather than built in, creating a machine even more versatile than the one envisaged here.

## THE WORLD OF TOMORROW

A SERIES OF 50

31

### FROST ELIMINATOR

Farmers and gardeners alike have often to deplore the destruction of their early crops by an unseasonable frost. Science may yet come to their rescue by providing huge portable frost dispellers of the type shown. High on a scaffolding would be mounted a great funnel, through which a current of warm air would be pumped by airplane propellers. The funnel could be turned by a handwheel in any suitable direction, so that the jet of warm air would be "aimed" like the discharge of a gun on any part of the garden or orchard that might require it.

**STEPHEN MITCHELL & SON**

ISSUED BY THE IMPERIAL TOBACCO CO. (OF GREAT BRITAIN & IRELAND), LTD.

MITCHELL'S CIGARETTES

FROST ELIMINATOR

31
FROST ELIMINATOR

When this card was written, oil-burning orchard heaters had been introduced in California to combat frost, but they were soon banned on ecological grounds. Smaller gas heaters now provide the foreseen frost protection, not just in American fruit fields but also in these Swiss vineyards.

# THE WORLD OF TOMORROW

A SERIES OF 50

32

NORTH SEA RECLAMATION

Good work has already been done in reclaiming shallow bays and inlets of the sea in order to convert their floor into fertile land. (The most remarkable so far is the draining of the Zuyder Zee.) The illustration shows a more ambitious scheme for reclaiming the whole floor of the North Sea on similar lines. Dykes would have to be run from Scotland to Norway and across the English Channel, and the area enclosed would be drained, laid with soil and adapted for cultivation. This would add many hundred square miles to the land surfaces of the world; it would also have a startling effect in that Great Britain would cease to be an island!

**STEPHEN MITCHELL & SON**

ISSUED BY THE IMPERIAL TOBACCO CO.
(OF GREAT BRITAIN & IRELAND), LTD.

NORTH SEA RECLAMATION

32
NORTH SEA RECLAMATION

Dykes from 'Scotland to Norway and across the English Channel'? The enclosed area 'drained' and
'laid with soil'? The writer's faith in our ability to restrain the raging sea proved to be unfounded, leaving 'the Zuyder Zee'
(now IJsselmeer) in The Netherlands still the most impressive area of North Sea reclamation to date.

MITCHELL'S CIGARETTES

RECLAMATION OF SEA-FLOOR

## 33
### RECLAMATION OF SEA-FLOOR

Mid-ocean reclamation remains an impractical proposition, but coastal 'Zuyder Zee'-style projects
now include Dubai's Palm and World residential developments. In Hong Kong, the reclaimed site for the recently
completed Chek Lap Kok airport, shown here, bears an uncanny resemblance to the card's illustration.

THE WORLD OF TOMORROW

A SERIES OF 50

34

GIBRALTAR DAM

Every second over a hundred thousand cubic yards of water flow from the Atlantic Ocean into the Mediterranean Sea through the Straits of Gibraltar. By the construction of a huge dam, traversed by canals through which shipping could pass, this mighty inflow could be diverted into turbines and its power transformed into useful energy. After passing through the turbines, the water could be used for irrigation schemes in the Sahara, thus making the arid desert to blossom as the rose. Any surplus water would soon evaporate in the fierce rays of the sun, so that the flow through the Straits would remain undiminished.

STEPHEN MITCHELL & SON

ISSUED BY THE IMPERIAL TOBACCO CO. (OF GREAT BRITAIN & IRELAND) LTD.

MITCHELL'S CIGARETTES

GIBRALTAR DAM

34
GIBRALTAR DAM

The Straits of Gibraltar remain as they ever were. A dam to harness the 'mighty inflow' from the Atlantic, 'traversed by canals through which shipping could pass', proved to be too tall an order, as did the desalination plant needed to encourage the Sahara 'to blossom as the rose'.

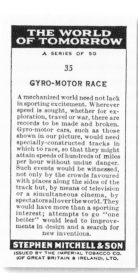

A mechanized world need not lack in sporting excitement. Wherever speed is sought, whether for exploration, travel or war, there are records to be made and broken. Gyro-motor cars, such as those shown in our picture, would need specially-constructed tracks in which to race, so that they might attain speeds of hundreds of miles per hour without undue danger. Such events would be witnessed, not only by the crowds favoured with places along the sides of the track but, by means of television or a simultaneous cinema, by spectators all over the world. They would have more than a sporting interest; attempts to go "one better" would lead to improvements in design and a search for new inventions.

**STEPHEN MITCHELL & SON**

ISSUED BY THE IMPERIAL TOBACCO CO.
(OF GREAT BRITAIN & IRELAND), LTD.

MITCHELL'S CIGARETTES

GYRO-MOTOR RACE

35
GYRO-MOTOR RACE

Although the technology dates back to 1852, gyros were being used to stabilize in-line two-wheeled 'gyrocars'
as recently as the 1960s. The slim motorcycle layout and light weight enabled higher speeds and lower cornering angles,
allowing the steep banking depicted on the card but now outlawed on the Grand Prix circuit.

THE WORLD
OF TOMORROW

A SERIES OF 50

36

BIRDMAN

A new form of sport has recently been developed by an enterprising American aviator, Clem Sohn. Equipped with artificial wings strapped between his arms and his body and a "tail" joining his legs, and provided with a parachute for landing, he jumps from an airplane in flight. Spreading his wings and "tail," and controlling them with movements of his arms and legs, he swoops in any direction he chooses. This novel form of gliding might be taken up widely within a few years, so that our skies would be filled, as our bays are filled with swimmers and our roads with cyclists, with birdmen drifting down on the wind or gracefully soaring aloft.

STEPHEN MITCHELL & SON

ISSUED BY THE IMPERIAL TOBACCO CO. (OF GREAT BRITAIN & IRELAND), LTD.

MITCHELL'S CIGARETTES

BIRDMAN

36
BIRDMAN

No sooner did man walk the earth than he began to dream of flying above it.
In the wake of Leonardo da Vinci came the entertaining Mr Sohn. According to the card, he still needed an aircraft to take to the skies, whereas all the modern hang-glider needs is a mountain or hill.

## THE WORLD OF TOMORROW

A SERIES OF 50

37

### ROBOT OR MECHANICAL MAN

The word "robot" was first used in M. Karel Capek's play *R.U.R.* to describe artificial men built up in the laboratory. To-day it is more often used for machines made more or less in a human form; such devices attract much attention at exhibitions. The one shown is a Russian invention; it can handle and carry loads far too heavy for a man. Spectacular though these machines are, it is doubtful whether they will be of much practical use, but they may none the less be used as a "stunt" for impressing people or even frightening them. Any burglar who encountered one of these mechanical watchmen would probably beat a hasty retreat!

**STEPHEN MITCHELL & SON**

ISSUED BY THE IMPERIAL TOBACCO CO.
(OF GREAT BRITAIN & IRELAND) LTD.

MITCHELL'S CIGARETTES

ROBOT OR MECHANICAL MAN

## 37
### ROBOT OR MECHANICAL MAN

Honda's Asimo could walk and talk at an early age. Now twenty, he can run, climb stairs, fetch and carry, and shake hands. That said, it is in the world's factories and hospitals that robotics

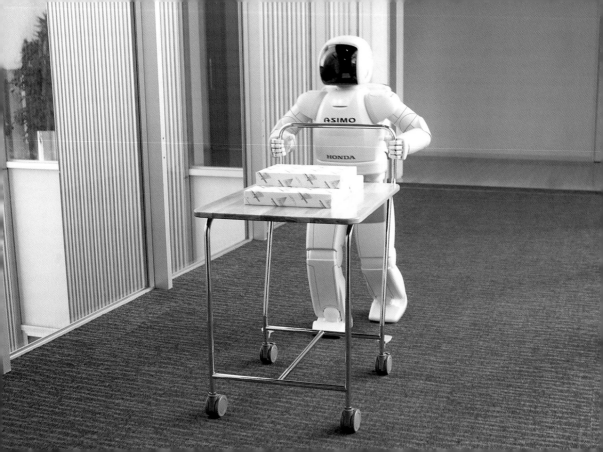

MITCHELL'S CIGARETTES

THOUGHT-DETECTING MACHINE

## 38
## THOUGHT-DETECTING MACHINE

While the polygraph, or lie detector, shown simply flagged anxiety, the modern scanner identifies brain activity corresponding to different thoughts, with up to 70 per cent accuracy. As well as bringing the predicted benefits in criminal investigations, it is helping drive the development of devices that are operated mentally rather than manually, including artificial limbs.

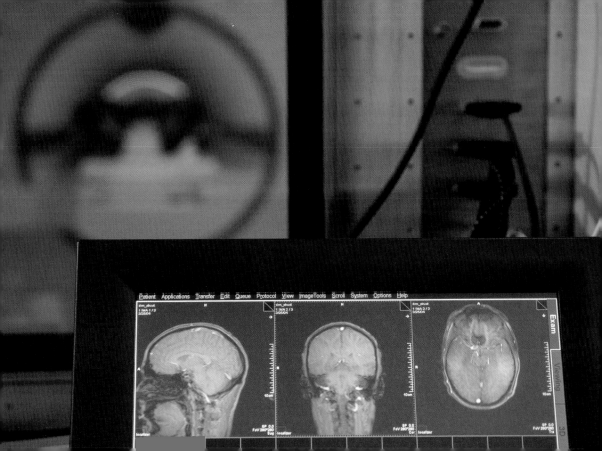

## THE WORLD OF TOMORROW

A SERIES OF 50

39

### INVASION FROM THE AIR

The army of Soviet Russia, in co-operation with its air force, has recently developed a new method of warfare. By means of parachutes whole battalions of men, with their arms and equipment, have been dropped simultaneously to the ground from flights of airplanes: even field-guns and tanks are said to have been thus carried. This novel method of attack may become a regular feature of warfare, enabling armies to launch an invasion right in the heart of the enemy's country without having to face its coastal or frontier defences. The invaders would be in a splendid position for launching a surprise attack from the rear, for seizing vital centres, or for cutting communications.

**STEPHEN MITCHELL & SON**

ISSUED BY THE IMPERIAL TOBACCO CO. (OF GREAT BRITAIN & IRELAND) LTD.

MITCHELL'S CIGARETTES

INVASION FROM THE AIR

39
INVASION FROM THE AIR

The mass parachute drop became a widely deployed tactic sooner than the writer might have imagined, and it remains one today. There is, however, a challenger on the horizon: a 'Personal Flying Wing', which enables a paratrooper to glide for some 40 kilometres (25 miles) after his jump.

## THE WORLD OF TOMORROW

A SERIES OF 50

40

### ANTI-GAS ARMOUR

The poison gas of the future may kill not merely when it is inhaled, but when it touches any part of the body. For protection against such a weapon ordinary respirators would be useless; protective clothing would be needed, combined with gauntlets and a face mask to protect every part of the body. Such a device may seem clumsy, but it need not encumber the wearer as does the present-day respirator. The mask might be formed of transparent material strengthened by a wire framework, and would be large enough to enable the head to be turned freely. (*Photograph by courtesy of London Film Productions, Ltd., from the film "Things to Come"*).

**STEPHEN MITCHELL & SON**

ISSUED BY THE IMPERIAL TOBACCO CO. (OF GREAT BRITAIN & IRELAND) LTD.

MITCHELL'S CIGARETTES

ANTI-GAS ARMOUR

### 40
### ANTI-GAS ARMOUR

With the gas and chemical weapons of the First World War still a vivid memory, this card foresees substances that kill on contact as well as via inhalation. Regrettably, such fears remain well founded, and today's soldiers are still schooled in the use of nuclear, biological and chemical warfare kit.

## THE WORLD OF TOMORROW

A SERIES OF 50

41

### ANTI-GAS RAY

Science has made war terrible by devising new weapons for attack; the scientists of the future must concentrate on finding defences against which these would be powerless. Our picture shows a possibility of science applied to defensive warfare—a ray or electrical discharge which, directed into the heart of a gas-cloud, would disperse it, neutralize it, or condense it into a harmless liquid. Other rays may be discovered to stop an airplane engine, ignite its stores of petrol, explode its bombs, or even kill its pilot before he could reach our shores and hurl his deadly missiles upon us.

**STEPHEN MITCHELL & SON**

ISSUED BY THE IMPERIAL TOBACCO CO. (OF GREAT BRITAIN & IRELAND), LTD.

MITCHELL'S CIGARETTES

ANTI-GAS RAY

41
ANTI-GAS RAY

The talk of a defensive 'ray or electrical discharge' is reminiscent of the sci-fi weapons envisaged in Ronald Reagan's 'Star Wars' programme of the 1980s. While most are still pie in the sky, the Tactical High-Energy Laser is a reality. Armed with a beam that can destroy enemy fire, it is in the final stages of development with the US Army.

# THE WORLD OF TOMORROW

A SERIES OF 50

42

## ROCKET POST

Already *Rockets* have been successfully used, not only for propelling cars, cycles, and sledges, but also for conveying mail. With further advances in their construction so as to make their flight more reliable, they would be very useful for carrying letters from ships to land, and also across belts of water such as the Straits of Dover. The letters would be placed in the metal rocket-body, protected both from the heat of the flaming gases and from the shock of landing. The rocket would be aimed like a gun, and kept on its course by vanes like those of an airplane bomb.

## STEPHEN MITCHELL & SON

ISSUED BY THE IMPERIAL TOBACCO CO.
(OF GREAT BRITAIN & IRELAND), LTD.

MITCHELL'S CIGARETTES

ROCKET POST

42
ROCKET POST

As foreseen, fast communications have become important, but this charming idea really does appear to have gone up in smoke. The ticker tape, telex and fax have come and gone. Today we can send images and messages by email; in place of ballistics we have buttons.

MITCHELL'S CIGARETTES

CATHODE ROCKET SPACE-SHIP

## 43
### CATHODE ROCKET SPACE-SHIP

The speculation proved to be far more accurate than the visualization.
Since their early days, spacecraft have indeed sprouted 'metal vanes' to harness solar energy,
although this is used primarily to supply internal power rather than external propulsion.

## THE WORLD OF TOMORROW

A SERIES OF 50

44

### LAUNCHING A SPACE-SHIP

Many problems would have to be solved to make flight possible beyond the earth's atmosphere; though at present the space-ship is only a vision of the future, there is no need to suppose that these problems are insoluble. Such a vessel would probably need a great sloping way from which to start, solid enough to resist the terrific back-blast of incandescent gases from its rocket tubes as they drive it majestically aloft. Ships returning to earth would probably drop into unfrequented parts of the ocean, where they could arrive safely and do little damage; a fleet of tugs would then haul them to the refitting shops, where they would be made ready for another flight.

**STEPHEN MITCHELL & SON**

ISSUED BY THE IMPERIAL TOBACCO CO.
(OF GREAT BRITAIN & IRELAND) LTD.

MITCHELL'S CIGARETTES

LAUNCHING A SPACE-SHIP

44
LAUNCHING A SPACE-SHIP

An upright launch pad proved to be better than a sloping one, but other projections have come to pass. For many years returning craft were ditched in 'unfrequented parts of the ocean', as suggested, and NASA does have 'refitting shops', where its Space Shuttle is 'made ready for another flight'.

## THE WORLD OF TOMORROW

A SERIES OF 50

45

### SPACE-GUN

In imaginative stories and films, space-guns have been suggested large enough to hurl a shell, possibly containing living beings, to the moon. It is doubtful whether this is practicable—to pass beyond the earth's attraction the shell would need a muzzle velocity of seven miles a second, and the shock of such a discharge would probably be enough to destroy its crew. None the less, such a gun might be very useful for sending observational expeditions beyond the atmosphere, or for giving a swift "start off" to an interplanetary rocket-ship or a vessel propelled by the radiation pressure of the sun. It would need an immense gantry to lower the space-shell and explosives into it. *(Photograph by courtesy of London Film Productions, Ltd., from the film " Things to Come ").*

**STEPHEN MITCHELL & SON**

ISSUED BY THE IMPERIAL TOBACCO CO. (OF GREAT BRITAIN & IRELAND), LTD.

MITCHELL'S CIGARETTES

SPACE-GUN

45
SPACE-GUN

Manned spacecraft developed as fuelled rockets rather than fired shells, so there has never been a gun of the sort depicted here. However, the card title hints at airborne weaponry that is very much a part of modern warfare, as this fearsome salvo fired by Iranian forces shows.

INSIDE A SPACE-SHIP

## 46
### INSIDE A SPACE-SHIP

One thing spacecraft have always lacked is space. There is certainly no room for 'well-padded chairs suspended from huge springs'. In fact, in early craft there was barely room to move. The interior of a space station is more roomy, but still nothing like the commodious cabin pictured on the card.

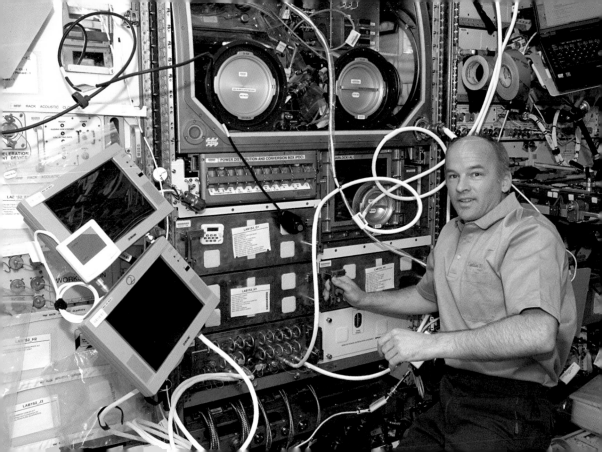

## THE WORLD OF TOMORROW

A SERIES OF 50

47

### SPACE-SUITS

For landing on other planets, and for repairing space-ships, explorers beyond the atmosphere would need space-suits. These would have to be air-tight and carry generous supplies of oxygen, and also, perhaps, of food and water. They would need to be strong enough to resist the pressure of the air within and accidental blows from without, for any leakage would be fatal. At the same time they would have to be flexible enough to enable their wearers to walk about and to handle objects. They would be electrically heated, and probably provided with wireless telephones.

**STEPHEN MITCHELL & SON**

ISSUED BY THE IMPERIAL TOBACCO CO.
(OF GREAT BRITAIN & IRELAND), LTD.

MITCHELL'S CIGARETTES

SPACE-SUITS

47
SPACE-SUITS

The writer accurately prescribes airtight suits and oxygen supplies for would-be space travellers. He even foresees the need for flexibility, so that the wearer can 'walk about' and 'handle objects'. Oddly, the armoured outfits in the drawing look anything but flexible.

# THE WORLD OF TOMORROW

A SERIES OF 50

48

## NEW STYLE OBSERVATORY

We owe all our modern inventions and technical devices to advances in scientific knowledge. At the same time these inventions and improvements make further advances in knowledge possible by giving the scientist new materials to experiment with, new forces to handle, new devices to use, and improved laboratories and observatories in which to work. A recent advance in observatory construction is shown in our illustration: the dome which contains the great telescope is situated at the top of a concrete building, protected against vibration and lifted above the disturbances which might be found at a lower level. The great Professor Einstein, the discoverer of relativity, at one time worked in such an observatory.

**STEPHEN MITCHELL & SON**

ISSUED BY THE IMPERIAL TOBACCO CO.
(OF GREAT BRITAIN & IRELAND), LTD.

MITCHELL'S CIGARETTES

NEW STYLE OBSERVATORY

48
NEW STYLE OBSERVATORY

The card shows Erich Mendelsohn's recently completed observatory, the Einstein Tower in Potsdam, Germany, which incorporated a tower to keep the telescope above 'disturbances'. Hawaii's Mauna Kea station sits at altitude for much the same reason: 4205 metres (13,796 feet) up, it is clear of clouds and atmospheric pollution.

MITCHELL'S CIGARETTES

GIANT TELESCOPE

49
GIANT TELESCOPE
No one could have foreseen the development of the orbiting Hubble Space Telescope, which transmits images free of atmospheric distortion. Here is its terrestrial equivalent, the Hobby-Eberly Telescope at Mount Fowlkes in Texas. Its ninety-one-piece, 11-metre-diameter (36 feet) reflective surface is the largest primary mirror on Earth.

## THE WORLD OF TOMORROW

A SERIES OF 50

50

### WEATHER CONTROL

Though at present we cannot even foretell the weather, let alone control it, there is no need to suppose that we shall always be so helpless. The picture shows a possible method of producing rain artificially. Electrified globes at the top of great towers would attract the clouds; failing natural clouds, streams of water pumped to their top would be evaporated on electrically-heated plates to form water vapour. Discharges of powerful electric sparks, like an artificial thunderstorm, would cool the air, condense the clouds, and bring their contents to earth as rain. In the meantime, a series of automatically-controlled motor-sowers might turn up the soil and scatter the seeds.

### STEPHEN MITCHELL & SON

ISSUED BY THE IMPERIAL TOBACCO CO. (OF GREAT BRITAIN & IRELAND) LTD.

MITCHELL'S CIGARETTES

WEATHER CONTROL

50
WEATHER CONTROL

Today we can induce rain by spraying chemicals on clouds. But the card's sparks and steelwork beg comparison with HAARP (High-frequency Active Auroral Research Program), a US government facility in Gakona, Alaska. Here, scientists fire high-frequency radio waves into the ionosphere and study the results.

## Picture credits

All Mitchell's cigarette cards are reproduced with kind permission of Imperial Tobacco Limited unless otherwise stated. Photographs are referred to by the number of the card opposite which they appear.

First published 2007 by Merrell Publishers Limited

Head office
81 Southwark Street
London SE1 0HX

New York office
49 West 24th Street, 8th Floor
New York, NY 10010

merrellpublishers.com

British Library Cataloguing-in-Publication data:
Marcantonio, Alfredo
Prophets of zoom
1. Stephen Mitchell & Son (Firm) 2. Cigarette cards –
Scotland 3. Cigarette cards – Scotland – Pictorial
works 4. Technological forecasting – Scotland
5. Technological forecasting – Scotland – Pictorial
works 6. Twentieth century – Forecasts 7. Twentieth
century – Forecasts – Pictorial works
I. Title
741.6'85

ISBN-13: 978-1-8589-4401-2
ISBN-10: 1-8589-4401-5

Produced by Merrell Publishers Limited
Designed by Leo Marcantonio
Copy-edited by Charlotte Rundall
Proof-read by Kate Michell
Printed and bound in Singapore